In the corner today, we're talking about feeling angry.
This way to Kids Corner

When I feel angry, I feel like

a volcano about
to erupt,

a pot about
to boil over,

a bull running around
in a china shop.

When I feel angry, I feel like

a charging rhinoceros,

a balloon about
to pop,

an exploding
rocket!

I stamp my feet
when I feel angry.

But it doesn't
help me
very much.

I throw my toys
when I feel angry.

But I'm really
upset if I break
something.

When I feel angry
with my brother,
I say I won't speak
to him ever again.

But I always forgive him in the end.

When I feel angry with my friend,
I call her names
and I say I won't play with her.

But I always feel
sorry later on.

A lot of things make people feel angry. When Mom is tired after work, and we're making lots of noise,

she feels
really angry!

When my sister is building a model,
and she just can't get it right,

she feels angry.

When my friend Johnny
gets into trouble
for something he didn't do,

he feels angry.

Sometimes I make people feel angry when I—

forget
my manners
and don't behave,

or when I'm selfish
and won't share my toys.

I make people feel angry

if I yell and throw things
when I lose a game,

or if I make fun
of someone
who can’t do something.

I make my teacher feel angry
if I tease other kids,

or if I copy
someone else's
answers on a test.

Everyone feels angry sometimes.
But when I start to feel angry,

it helps if I count
to ten before I speak.

It helps if I run
until I'm tired
or kick a ball
really hard.

It helps if I tell my problems
to the dog.
He seems to understand.

It helps if I think of something nice.
Then I often forget
why I feel angry.

But the thing
that helps most
is talking
about how I feel.

What do you do
when you feel angry?

Things to Do in the Kids Corner

Make a "Mad-to-Glad Card." On an index card, write a list or draw pictures of nice things you like to think about. When you feel angry, look at your card and think about the nice things on it. You'll go from mad to glad in no time!

Work with a friend. Make letter cards for *a, n, g, r,* and *y*. Pick a card, then say as many words as you can that start with that letter. Take turns drawing cards and naming words.

Draw a picture about a time when you were angry. Write a caption for your picture. Share your work with a friend. Tell your friend what you did to feel better.

Make up a silly sentence. Make each word start with the letters in the word *angry*, like *Anteaters never gulp raspberry yogurt.* Write your sentence on a piece of paper. Draw a picture to go with it.

Only two words in the book have exactly ten letters. Find them. Now challenge a friend to find them and read them to you.

Other Books to Read

Looking for Dad, by Ellen Frances (Sundance, 1999). John is angry when his mom plans to marry Steve. Why didn't anyone ask him how he felt? His search for the perfect dad has a surprising ending. Other Sundance books you might like to read are *The Trouble with Parents*, by Dianne Bates; and *Green with Red Spots Horrible*, by Jen McVeity. *64 pages*

Thomas Had a Temper, by Nicki Saltis (a Sundance *AlphaKids Guided Reader*, 1999). A young boy named Thomas learns to control his temper when he meets Kate, a girl who has a bad temper, too. Together, they learn to play without losing their tempers. *16 pages*

Alexander and the Terrible, Horrible, No Good, Very Bad Day, by Judith Viorst (Simon and Schuster, 1987). From waking up with gum in his hair to lima beans for supper, Alexander finds there are days when nothing goes right. *32 pages*

Amber Brown Sees Red, by Paula Danziger (Scholastic Books, 1997). Amber's life is in for some big changes when her mom gets engaged. Now her dad is returning to the United States and wants her to live with him. Her parents argue every time they talk on the phone. Caught in the middle, Amber Brown sees RED! *116 pages*

The Flunking of Joshua T. Bates, by Susan Shreve (Random House, 1997). What could be worse than repeating third grade? When nine-year-old Joshua T. Bates is faced with that horrible situation, he gets angry. *82 pages*